MznLnx

Missing Links Exam Preps

Exam Prep for

Sales Forecasting Management: A Demand Management Approach

Mentzer, Moon, 2nd Edition

The MznLnx Exam Prep is your link from the texbook and lecture to your exams.
The MznLnx Exam Preps are unauthorized and comprehensive reviews of your textbooks.

All material provided by MznLnx and Rico Publications (c) 2010
Textbook publishers and textbook authors do not particpate in or contribute to these reviews.

MznLnx

Rico Publications

Exam Prep for Sales Forecasting Management: A Demand Management Approach
2nd Edition
Mentzer, Moon

Publisher: Raymond Houge
Assistant Editor: Michael Rouger
Text and Cover Designer: Lisa Buckner
Marketing Manager: Sara Swagger
Project Manager, Editorial Production: Jerry Emerson
Art Director: Vernon Lowerui

Product Manager: Dave Mason
Editorial Assitant: Rachel Guzmanji
Pedagogy: Debra Long
Cover Image: Jim Reed/Getty Images
Text and Cover Printer: City Printing, Inc.
Compositor: Media Mix, Inc.

(c) 2010 Rico Publications

ALL RIGHTS RESERVED. No part of this work covered by the copyright may be reproduced or used in any form or by an means--graphic, electronic, or mechanical, including photocopying, recording, taping, Web distribution, information storage, and retrieval systems, or in any other manner--without the written permission of the publisher.

For more information about our products, contact us at:
Dave.Mason@RicoPublications.com

For permission to use material from this text or product, submit a request online to:
Dave.Mason@RicoPublications.com

Printed in the United States
ISBN:

Contents

CHAPTER 1
Managing the Sales Forecasting Process — 1

CHAPTER 2
Sales Forecasting Performance Measurement — 7

CHAPTER 3
Time Series Forecasting Techniques — 12

CHAPTER 4
Regression Analysis — 15

CHAPTER 5
Qualitative Sales Forecasting — 21

CHAPTER 6
Sales Forecasting Systems — 27

CHAPTER 7
Benchmark Studies: The Surveys — 30

CHAPTER 8
Benchmark Studies: World-Class Forecasting — 32

CHAPTER 9
Benchmark Studies: Conducting a Forecasting Audit — 34

CHAPTER 10
Managing the Sales Forecasting Function — 36

ANSWER KEY — 40

TO THE STUDENT

COMPREHENSIVE

The *MznLnx* Exam Prep series is designed to help you pass your exams. Editors at MznLnx review your textbooks and then prepare these practice exams to help you master the textbook material. Unlike study guides, workbooks, and practice tests provided by the texbook publisher and textbook authors, *MznLnx* gives you **all** of the material in each chapter in exam form, not just samples, so you can be sure to nail your exam.

MECHANICAL

The MznLnx Exam Prep series creates exams that will help you learn the subject matter as well as test you on your understanding. Each question is designed to help you master the concept. Just working through the exams, you gain an understanding of the subject--its a simple mechanical process that produces success.

INTEGRATED STUDY GUIDE AND REVIEW

MznLnx is not just a set of exams designed to test you, its also a comprehensive review of the subject content. Each exam question is also a review of the concept, making sure that you will get the answer correct without having to go to other sources of material. You learn as you go! Its the easiest way to pass an exam.

HUMOR

Studying can be tedious and dry. MznLnx's instructional design includes moderate humor within the exam questions on occassion, to break the tedium and revitalize the brain

Chapter 1. Managing the Sales Forecasting Process   1

1. The _____ is a systematic, interactive forecasting method which relies on a panel of independent experts. The carefully selected experts answer questionnaires in two or more rounds. After each round, a facilitator provides an anonymous summary of the experts' forecasts from the previous round as well as the reasons they provided for their judgments.
   a. Futurist
   b. 180SearchAssistant
   c. Power III
   d. Delphi method

2. In economics, _____ is the desire to own something and the ability to pay for it. The term _____ signifies the ability or the willingness to buy a particular commodity at a given point of time .

   a. Discretionary spending
   b. Market system
   c. Market dominance
   d. Demand

3. In economics, _____' is the art or science of controlling economic demand to avoid a recession. In natural resources management and environmental policy more generally, it refers to policies to control consumer demand for environmentally sensitive or harmful goods such as water and energy. Within manufacturing firms the term is used to describe the activities of demand forecasting, planning and order fulfillment.
   a. Power III
   b. 6-3-5 Brainwriting
   c. 180SearchAssistant
   d. Demand management

4. _____ is a term in economics, where demand for one good or service occurs as a result of demand for another. This may occur as the former is a part of production of the second. For example, demand for coal leads to _____ for mining, as coal must be mined for coal to be consumed.
   a. 6-3-5 Brainwriting
   b. 180SearchAssistant
   c. Power III
   d. Derived demand

5. A _____ or logistics network is the system of organizations, people, technology, activities, information and resources involved in moving a product or service from supplier to customer. _____ activities transform natural resources, raw materials and components into a finished product that is delivered to the end customer. In sophisticated _____ systems, used products may re-enter the _____ at any point where residual value is recyclable.

Chapter 1. Managing the Sales Forecasting Process

   a. Purchasing
   b. Supply chain network
   c. Demand chain management
   d. Supply chain

6. _____ is the process of estimation in unknown situations. Prediction is a similar, but more general term. Both can refer to estimation of time series, cross-sectional or longitudinal data.
   a. 180SearchAssistant
   b. Forecasting
   c. Power III
   d. 6-3-5 Brainwriting

7. _____ in organizations and public policy is both the organizational process of creating and maintaining a plan; and the psychological process of thinking about the activities required to create a desired goal on some scale. As such, it is a fundamental property of intelligent behavior. This thought process is essential to the creation and refinement of a plan, or integration of it with other plans, that is, it combines forecasting of developments with the preparation of scenarios of how to react to them.
   a. 6-3-5 Brainwriting
   b. 180SearchAssistant
   c. Power III
   d. Planning

8. Customer _____ consists of the processes a company uses to track and organize its contacts with its current and prospective customers. CRelationship management software is used to support these processes; information about customers and customer interactions can be entered, stored and accessed by employees in different company departments. Typical CRelationship management goals are to improve services provided to customers, and to use customer contact information for targeted marketing.
   a. Marketing
   b. Relationship management
   c. Green marketing
   d. Product bundling

9. _____ is defined by the American _____ Association as the activity, set of institutions, and processes for creating, communicating, delivering, and exchanging offerings that have value for customers, clients, partners, and society at large. The term developed from the original meaning which referred literally to going to market, as in shopping, or going to a market to sell goods or services.

_____ practice tends to be seen as a creative industry, which includes advertising, distribution and selling.

a. Marketing myopia
b. Customer acquisition management
c. Product naming
d. Marketing

10. In economics, business, retail, and accounting, a _____ is the value of money that has been used up to produce something, and hence is not available for use anymore. In economics, a _____ is an alternative that is given up as a result of a decision. In business, the _____ may be one of acquisition, in which case the amount of money expended to acquire it is counted as _____.
   a. Variable cost
   b. Cost
   c. Transaction cost
   d. Fixed costs

11. _____ is the management of the flow of goods, information and other resources, including energy and people, between the point of origin and the point of consumption in order to meet the requirements of consumers (frequently, and originally, military organizations.) _____ involves the integration of information, transportation, inventory, warehousing, material-handling, and packaging. _____ is a channel of the supply chain which adds the value of time and place utility.
   a. Power III
   b. Logistics
   c. 6-3-5 Brainwriting
   d. 180SearchAssistant

12. _____ refers to a business or organization attempting to acquire goods or services to accomplish the goals of the enterprise. Though there are several organizations that attempt to set standards in the _____ process, processes can vary greatly between organizations. Typically the word '_____' is not used interchangeably with the word 'procurement', since procurement typically includes Expediting, Supplier Quality, and Traffic and Logistics (T'L) in addition to _____.
   a. Drop shipping
   b. Supply chain
   c. Supply network
   d. Purchasing

13. In probability theory and statistics, _____ indicates the strength and direction of a linear relationship between two random variables. That is in contrast with the usage of the term in colloquial speech, denoting any relationship, not necessarily linear. In general statistical usage, _____ or co-relation refers to the departure of two random variables from independence.

Chapter 1. Managing the Sales Forecasting Process

a. Mean
b. Probability
c. Correlation
d. Frequency distribution

14. _____ refers to the process by which tissues of dead organisms break down into simpler forms of matter. Such a breakdown of dead organisms is essential for new growth and development of living organisms because it recycles the finite chemical constituents and frees up the limited physical space in the biome. Bodies of living organisms begin to decompose shortly after death.
   a. 6-3-5 Brainwriting
   b. Power III
   c. Decomposition
   d. 180SearchAssistant

15. In statistics and image processing, to smooth a data set is to create an approximating function that attempts to capture important patterns in the data, while leaving out noise or other fine-scale structures/rapid phenomena. Many different algorithms are used in _____. One of the most common algorithms is the 'moving average', often used to try to capture important trends in repeated statistical surveys.
   a. 6-3-5 Brainwriting
   b. 180SearchAssistant
   c. Smoothing
   d. Power III

16. In mathematics, an _____, or central tendency of a data set refers to a measure of the 'middle' or 'expected' value of the data set. There are many different descriptive statistics that can be chosen as a measurement of the central tendency of the data items.

An _____ is a single value that is meant to typify a list of values.

   a. ADTECH
   b. Average
   c. ACNielsen
   d. AMAX

17. In statistics, _____ is a collective name for techniques for the modeling and analysis of numerical data consisting of values of a dependent variable and of one or more independent variables The dependent variable in the regression equation is modeled as a function of the independent variables, corresponding parameters, and an error term. The error term is treated as a random variable.

Chapter 1. Managing the Sales Forecasting Process

a. Stepwise regression
b. Multicollinearity
c. Variance inflation factor
d. Regression analysis

18. The _____ is the group of customers and/or consumers that a business serves. In the most situations, a large part of this group is made up of repeat customers with a high ratio of purchase over time. These customers are the main source of consumer spending.
   a. Psychological pricing
   b. Customer base
   c. Supplier diversity
   d. First-mover advantage

19. _____ refer to a collection of facts usually collected as the result of experience, observation or experiment or a set of premises. This may consist of numbers, words particularly as measurements or observations of a set of variables. _____ are often viewed as a lowest level of abstraction from which information and knowledge are derived.
   a. Data
   b. Pearson product-moment correlation coefficient
   c. Sample size
   d. Mean

20. In economics, an externality or spillover of an economic transaction is an impact on a party that is not directly involved in the transaction. In such a case, prices do not reflect the full costs or benefits in production or consumption of a product or service. A positive impact is called an _____ benefit, while a negative impact is called an _____ cost.
   a. ADTECH
   b. AMAX
   c. ACNielsen
   d. External

21. _____ is one of the four elements of marketing mix. An organization or set of organizations (go-betweens) involved in the process of making a product or service available for use or consumption by a consumer or business user.

The other three parts of the marketing mix are product, pricing, and promotion.

a. Comparison-Shopping agent
b. Japan Advertising Photographers' Association
c. Better Living Through Chemistry
d. Distribution

Chapter 2. Sales Forecasting Performance Measurement

1. _____ is the process of estimation in unknown situations. Prediction is a similar, but more general term. Both can refer to estimation of time series, cross-sectional or longitudinal data.
    a. Power III
    b. 180SearchAssistant
    c. 6-3-5 Brainwriting
    d. Forecasting

2. In statistics, _____ has two related meanings:

    - the arithmetic _____
    - the expected value of a random variable, which is also called the population _____.

    It is sometimes stated that the '_____' _____s average. This is incorrect if '_____' is taken in the specific sense of 'arithmetic _____' as there are different types of averages: the _____, median, and mode. For instance, average house prices almost always use the median value for the average. These three types of averages are all measures of locations.

    a. Heteroskedastic
    b. Mean
    c. Confidence interval
    d. Standard normal distribution

3. The _____ or simply average deviation of a data set is the average of the absolute deviations and is a summary statistic of statistical dispersion or variability. It is also called the mean absolute deviation, but this is easily confused with the median absolute deviation.

    The average absolute deviation of a set $\{x_1, x_2, ..., x_n\}$ is

    $$\frac{1}{n} \sum_{i=1}^{n} |x_i - m(X)|$$

    The choice of measure of central tendency, m(X), has a marked effect on the value of the average deviation.

    a. ADTECH
    b. Average absolute deviation,
    c. ACNielsen
    d. AMAX

4. In statistics, the _____ is a quantity used to measure how close forecasts or predictions are to the eventual outcomes. The _____ is given by

Chapter 2. Sales Forecasting Performance Measurement

$$\text{MAE} = \frac{1}{n}\sum_{i=1}^{n}|f_i - y_i| = \frac{1}{n}\sum_{i=1}^{n}|e_i|.$$

As the name suggests, the _____ is an average of the absolute errors $e_i = f_i - y_i$, where f_i is the prediction and y_i the true value. Note that alternative formulations may include relative frequencies as weight factors.

a. 180SearchAssistant
b. 6-3-5 Brainwriting
c. Power III
d. Mean absolute error

5. In statistics, the _____ or _____ of an estimator is one of many ways to quantify the amount by which an estimator differs from the true value of the quantity being estimated. As a loss function, _____ is called squared error loss. _____ measures the average of the square of the 'error.' The error is the amount by which the estimator differs from the quantity to be estimated.

a. 6-3-5 Brainwriting
b. 180SearchAssistant
c. Power III
d. Mean squared error

6. In statistical theory, a _____ is a specific type of estimator defined in a particular way. One use of the concept in statistical theory is that it allows a minimum-variance unbiased estimator to be derived from essentially any unbiased estimator, in contexts where no assumption is made about the form of the distribution and where estimation is for a function (such as the mean or variance) of the unknown distribution. Of even more importance is that the theory related to _____s allows a single theoretical framework to be used in non-parametric statistics to prove results for a wide range of test-statistics and estimators relating to the asymptotic normality and to the variance of such quantities.

a. AMAX
b. ADTECH
c. ACNielsen
d. U-statistic

7. In economics, business, retail, and accounting, a _____ is the value of money that has been used up to produce something, and hence is not available for use anymore. In economics, a _____ is an alternative that is given up as a result of a decision. In business, the _____ may be one of acquisition, in which case the amount of money expended to acquire it is counted as _____.

a. Transaction cost
b. Cost
c. Fixed costs
d. Variable cost

8. The _____ is a systematic, interactive forecasting method which relies on a panel of independent experts. The carefully selected experts answer questionnaires in two or more rounds. After each round, a facilitator provides an anonymous summary of the experts' forecasts from the previous round as well as the reasons they provided for their judgments.
   a. 180SearchAssistant
   b. Power III
   c. Futurist
   d. Delphi method

9. The general definition of an _____ is an evaluation of a person, organization, system, process, project or product. _____s are performed to ascertain the validity and reliability of information; also to provide an assessment of a system's internal control. The goal of an _____ is to express an opinion on the person/organization/system (etc) in question, under evaluation based on work done on a test basis.
   a. ACNielsen
   b. ADTECH
   c. AMAX
   d. Audit

10. _____ is the management of the flow of goods, information and other resources, including energy and people, between the point of origin and the point of consumption in order to meet the requirements of consumers (frequently, and originally, military organizations.) _____ involves the integration of information, transportation, inventory, warehousing, material-handling, and packaging. _____ is a channel of the supply chain which adds the value of time and place utility.
    a. Power III
    b. 6-3-5 Brainwriting
    c. Logistics
    d. 180SearchAssistant

11. _____ is defined by the American _____ Association as the activity, set of institutions, and processes for creating, communicating, delivering, and exchanging offerings that have value for customers, clients, partners, and society at large. The term developed from the original meaning which referred literally to going to market, as in shopping, or going to a market to sell goods or services.

    _____ practice tends to be seen as a creative industry, which includes advertising, distribution and selling.

Chapter 2. Sales Forecasting Performance Measurement

   a. Customer acquisition management
   b. Marketing myopia
   c. Product naming
   d. Marketing

12. _____, a business term, is a measure of how products and services supplied by a company meet or surpass customer expectation. It is seen as a key performance indicator within business and is part of the four perspectives of a Balanced Scorecard.

In a competitive marketplace where businesses compete for customers, _____ is seen as a key differentiator and increasingly has become a key element of business strategy.

   a. Psychological pricing
   b. Customer base
   c. Supplier diversity
   d. Customer satisfaction

13. A mutual _____ or stockholder is an individual or company (including a corporation) that legally owns one or more shares of stock in a joint stock company. A company's _____s collectively own that company. Thus, the typical goal of such companies is to enhance _____ value.
   a. 180SearchAssistant
   b. Shareholder
   c. Total shareholder return
   d. Power III

14. _____ is a business buzz term, which implies that the ultimate measure of a company's success is to enrich shareholders. It became popular during the 1980s, and is particularly associated with former CEO of General Electric, Jack Welch. In March 2009, Welch openly turned his back on the concept, calling shardeholder value 'the dumbest idea in the world'.
   a. 180SearchAssistant
   b. Power III
   c. 6-3-5 Brainwriting
   d. Shareholder value

15. A personal and cultural _____ is a relative ethic _____, an assumption upon which implementation can be extrapolated. A _____ system is a set of consistent _____s and measures that is soo not true. A principle _____ is a foundation upon which other _____s and measures of integrity are based.

a. Supreme Court of the United States
b. Value
c. Perceptual maps
d. Package-on-Package

Chapter 3. Time Series Forecasting Techniques

1. _____ is the process of estimation in unknown situations. Prediction is a similar, but more general term. Both can refer to estimation of time series, cross-sectional or longitudinal data.
   a. 6-3-5 Brainwriting
   b. 180SearchAssistant
   c. Power III
   d. Forecasting

2. In statistics and image processing, to smooth a data set is to create an approximating function that attempts to capture important patterns in the data, while leaving out noise or other fine-scale structures/rapid phenomena. Many different algorithms are used in _____. One of the most common algorithms is the 'moving average', often used to try to capture important trends in repeated statistical surveys.
   a. Power III
   b. 180SearchAssistant
   c. 6-3-5 Brainwriting
   d. Smoothing

3. In mathematics, an _____, or central tendency of a data set refers to a measure of the 'middle' or 'expected' value of the data set. There are many different descriptive statistics that can be chosen as a measurement of the central tendency of the data items.

   An _____ is a single value that is meant to typify a list of values.

   a. Average
   b. ACNielsen
   c. AMAX
   d. ADTECH

4. _____ refers to the process by which tissues of dead organisms break down into simpler forms of matter. Such a breakdown of dead organisms is essential for new growth and development of living organisms because it recycles the finite chemical constituents and frees up the limited physical space in the biome. Bodies of living organisms begin to decompose shortly after death.
   a. 180SearchAssistant
   b. Power III
   c. Decomposition
   d. 6-3-5 Brainwriting

5. _____ refer to a collection of facts usually collected as the result of experience, observation or experiment or a set of premises. This may consist of numbers, words particularly as measurements or observations of a set of variables. _____ are often viewed as a lowest level of abstraction from which information and knowledge are derived.

a. Pearson product-moment correlation coefficient
b. Mean
c. Sample size
d. Data

6. In statistics, a _____ rolling mean or running average, is a type of finite impulse response filter used to analyze a set of data points by creating a series of averages of different subsets of the full data set. A _____ is not a single number, but it is a set of numbers, each of which is the average of the corresponding subset of a larger set of data points. A _____ may also use unequal weights for each data value in the subset to emphasize particular values in the subset.
   a. Frequency distribution
   b. Confounding variables
   c. Moving average
   d. Statistics

7. In statistics, _____ is a technique that can be applied to time series data, either to produce smoothed data for presentation, or to make forecasts. The time series data themselves are a sequence of observations. The observed phenomenon may be an essentially random process, or it may be an orderly, but noisy, process.
   a. Exponential smoothing
   b. ACNielsen
   c. ADTECH
   d. AMAX

8. The term _____ usually refers to a weighted arithmetic mean, but weighted versions of other means can also be calculated, such as the weighted geometric mean and the weighted harmonic mean.

Given two school classes, one with 20 students, and one with 30 students, the grades in each class on a test were:

   Morning class = 62, 67, 71, 74, 76, 77, 78, 79, 79, 80, 80, 81, 81, 82, 83, 84, 86, 89, 93, 98

   Afternoon class = 81, 82, 83, 84, 85, 86, 87, 87, 88, 88, 89, 89, 89, 90, 90, 90, 90, 91, 91, 91, 92, 92, 93, 93, 94, 95, 96, 97, 98, 99

The straight average for the morning class is 80 and the straight average of the afternoon class is 90. The straight average of 80 and 90 is 85, the mean of the two class means.

a. 180SearchAssistant
b. 6-3-5 Brainwriting
c. Power III
d. Weighted average

Chapter 4. Regression Analysis

1. In statistics, _____ is a collective name for techniques for the modeling and analysis of numerical data consisting of values of a dependent variable and of one or more independent variables The dependent variable in the regression equation is modeled as a function of the independent variables, corresponding parameters, and an error term. The error term is treated as a random variable.
   a. Variance inflation factor
   b. Regression analysis
   c. Stepwise regression
   d. Multicollinearity

2. In probability theory and statistics, _____ indicates the strength and direction of a linear relationship between two random variables. That is in contrast with the usage of the term in colloquial speech, denoting any relationship, not necessarily linear. In general statistical usage, _____ or co-relation refers to the departure of two random variables from independence.
   a. Frequency distribution
   b. Mean
   c. Probability
   d. Correlation

3. The _____ is a systematic, interactive forecasting method which relies on a panel of independent experts. The carefully selected experts answer questionnaires in two or more rounds. After each round, a facilitator provides an anonymous summary of the experts' forecasts from the previous round as well as the reasons they provided for their judgments.
   a. 180SearchAssistant
   b. Futurist
   c. Power III
   d. Delphi method

4. _____ is the process of estimation in unknown situations. Prediction is a similar, but more general term. Both can refer to estimation of time series, cross-sectional or longitudinal data.
   a. 180SearchAssistant
   b. Power III
   c. 6-3-5 Brainwriting
   d. Forecasting

5. In statistics, _____ or explained randomness measures the proportion to which a mathematical model accounts for the variation (= apparent randomness) of a given data set. Often, variation is quantified as variance; then, the more specific term explained variance can be used.

The complementary part of the total variation/randomness/variance is called unexplained or residual.

Chapter 4. Regression Analysis

   a. ADTECH
   b. AMAX
   c. ACNielsen
   d. Explained variation

6. In mathematics, the _____ of a real-valued function f, defined on an interval [a, b] $\subset$ R is a measure of the one-dimensional arclength of the curve with parametric equation x → $f(x)$, for x ∈ [a,b]. The _____ of a continuously differentiable function can be given as the integral

$$V_b^a(f) = \int_a^b |f'(x)|\, dx.$$

The _____ of an arbitrary real valued function f defined on [a,b] is given by the more general formula

$$V_b^a(f) = \sup_P \sum_{i=0}^{n_P-1} |f(x_{i+1}) - f(x_i)|,$$

where the supremum runs over the set of all partitions P of the given interval.

The _____ of a real-valued integrable function f defined on a bounded domain $\Omega \subset \mathbb{R}^n$,

$$V(f, \Omega) := \sup\left\{\int_\Omega f \operatorname{div}\varphi : \varphi \in C_c^1(\Omega, \mathbb{R}^n),\ \|\varphi\|_{L^\infty(\Omega)} \leq 1\right\},$$

where $C_c^1(\Omega, \mathbb{R}^n)$ is the set of continuously differentiable vector functions of compact support contained in Ω (in particular Φ | $_{\delta\Omega}$ = 0), and $\|\ \|_{L^\infty}(\Omega)$ is the essential supremum norm.

   a. 6-3-5 Brainwriting
   b. Power III
   c. Total variation
   d. 180SearchAssistant

7. In statistics, _____ is used for two things;

- to construct a simple formula that will predict what value will occur for a quantity of interest when other related variables take given values.
- to allow a test to be made of whether a given variable does have an effect on a quantity of interest in situations where there may be many related variables.

In both cases, several sets of outcomes are available for the quantity of interest together with the related variables.

_____ is a form of regression analysis in which the relationship between one or more independent variables and another variable, called the dependent variable, is modelled by a least squares function, called a _____ equation. This function is a linear combination of one or more model parameters, called regression coefficients. A _____ equation with one independent variable represents a straight line when the predicted value (i.e. the dependant variable from the regression equation) is plotted against the independent variable: this is called a simple _____.

   a. Descriptive statistics
   b. Heteroskedastic
   c. Sample size
   d. Linear regression

8. _____ is a statistical phenomenon in which two or more predictor variables in a multiple regression model are highly correlated. In this situation the coefficient estimates may change erratically in response to small changes in the model or the data. _____ does not reduce the predictive power or reliability of the model as a whole; it only affects calculations regarding individual predictors.
   a. Regression analysis
   b. Variance inflation factor
   c. Stepwise regression
   d. Multicollinearity

9. _____s are used in open sentences. For instance, in the formula x + 1 = 5, x is a _____ which represents an 'unknown' number. _____s are often represented by letters of the Roman alphabet, or those of other alphabets, such as Greek, and use other special symbols.
   a. Variable
   b. Quantitative
   c. Book of business
   d. Personalization

Chapter 4. Regression Analysis

10. In statistics, the _____, R^2 is used in the context of statistical models whose main purpose is the prediction of future outcomes on the basis of other related information. It is the proportion of variability in a data set that is accounted for by the statistical model. It provides a measure of how well future outcomes are likely to be predicted by the model.

   a. Variance inflation factor
   b. Regression analysis
   c. Coefficient of determination
   d. Multicollinearity

11. _____ is a standard point of view or personal prejudice. especially when the tendency interferes with the ability to be impartial, unprejudiced, or objective. The term _____ed is used to describe an action, judgment, or other outcome influenced by a prejudged perspective.

   a. Power III
   b. Bias
   c. 180SearchAssistant
   d. 6-3-5 Brainwriting

12. In statistics, a result is called _____ if it is unlikely to have occurred by chance. 'A _____ difference' simply means there is statistical evidence that there is a difference; it does not mean the difference is necessarily large, important, or significant in the common meaning of the word.

   The significance level of a test is a traditional frequentist statistical hypothesis testing concept.

   a. Standard deviation
   b. Frequency distribution
   c. Randomization
   d. Statistically significant

13. In probability theory and statistics, the _____ of a random variable, probability distribution, or sample is a measure of statistical dispersion, averaging the squared distance of its possible values from the expected value (mean.) Whereas the mean is a way to describe the location of a distribution, the _____ is a way to capture its scale or degree of being spread out. The unit of _____ is the square of the unit of the original variable.

   a. Standard deviation
   b. Sample size
   c. Correlation
   d. Variance

Chapter 4. Regression Analysis

14. In statistics, the _____ is a method of detecting the severity of multicollinearity. More precisely, the _____ is an index which measures how much the variance of a coefficient (square of the standard deviation) is increased because of collinearity. Considering the following regression equation with k independent variables

$$Y = \beta_0 + \beta_1 X_1 + \beta_2 X_2 + ...$$

   a. Variance inflation factor
   b. Stepwise regression
   c. Multicollinearity
   d. Regression analysis

15. In economics, _____ is a rise in the general level of prices of goods and services in an economy over a period of time. The term '_____' once referred to increases in the money supply (monetary _____); however, economic debates about the relationship between money supply and price levels have led to its primary use today in describing price _____. Inflation can also be described as a decline in the real value of money--a loss of purchasing power in the medium of exchange which is also the monetary unit of account.
   a. ADTECH
   b. Inflation
   c. ACNielsen
   d. Industrial organization

16. _____ refer to a collection of facts usually collected as the result of experience, observation or experiment or a set of premises. This may consist of numbers, words particularly as measurements or observations of a set of variables. _____ are often viewed as a lowest level of abstraction from which information and knowledge are derived.
   a. Pearson product-moment correlation coefficient
   b. Sample size
   c. Mean
   d. Data

17. In statistics, a _____ is a mathematical relationship in which two occurrences have no causal connection, yet it may be inferred that they do, due to a certain third, unseen factor (referred to as a 'confounding factor' or 'lurking variable'.) The _____ gives an impression of a worthy link between two groups that is invalid when objectively examined.

The misleading correlation between two variables is produced through the operation of a third causal variable.

a. 180SearchAssistant
b. Power III
c. Spurious relationship
d. 6-3-5 Brainwriting

18. In statistics and image processing, to smooth a data set is to create an approximating function that attempts to capture important patterns in the data, while leaving out noise or other fine-scale structures/rapid phenomena. Many different algorithms are used in _____. One of the most common algorithms is the 'moving average', often used to try to capture important trends in repeated statistical surveys.
   a. 180SearchAssistant
   b. Smoothing
   c. Power III
   d. 6-3-5 Brainwriting

Chapter 5. Qualitative Sales Forecasting

1. The _____ is a systematic, interactive forecasting method which relies on a panel of independent experts. The carefully selected experts answer questionnaires in two or more rounds. After each round, a facilitator provides an anonymous summary of the experts' forecasts from the previous round as well as the reasons they provided for their judgments.
   a. 180SearchAssistant
   b. Delphi method
   c. Futurist
   d. Power III

2. In statistics, _____ is a collective name for techniques for the modeling and analysis of numerical data consisting of values of a dependent variable and of one or more independent variables The dependent variable in the regression equation is modeled as a function of the independent variables, corresponding parameters, and an error term. The error term is treated as a random variable.
   a. Variance inflation factor
   b. Stepwise regression
   c. Regression analysis
   d. Multicollinearity

3. _____ is the process of estimation in unknown situations. Prediction is a similar, but more general term. Both can refer to estimation of time series, cross-sectional or longitudinal data.
   a. 180SearchAssistant
   b. Power III
   c. 6-3-5 Brainwriting
   d. Forecasting

4. _____ is a standard point of view or personal prejudice. especially when the tendency interferes with the ability to be impartial, unprejudiced, or objective. The term _____ed is used to describe an action, judgment, or other outcome influenced by a prejudged perspective.
   a. 180SearchAssistant
   b. 6-3-5 Brainwriting
   c. Power III
   d. Bias

5. A _____ is a formal statement of a set of business goals, the reasons why they are believed attainable, and the plan for reaching those goals. It may also contain background information about the organization or team attempting to reach those goals.

The business goals may be defined for for-profit or for non-profit organizations.

a. Product marketing
b. Digital strategy
c. Logistics management
d. Business plan

6. In probability theory and statistics, _____ indicates the strength and direction of a linear relationship between two random variables. That is in contrast with the usage of the term in colloquial speech, denoting any relationship, not necessarily linear. In general statistical usage, _____ or co-relation refers to the departure of two random variables from independence.
   a. Mean
   b. Frequency distribution
   c. Probability
   d. Correlation

7. In accounting, _____ has a very specific meaning. It is an outflow of cash or other valuable assets from a person or company to another person or company. This outflow of cash is generally one side of a trade for products or services that have equal or better current or future value to the buyer than to the seller.
   a. ACNielsen
   b. Expense
   c. AMAX
   d. ADTECH

8. _____ is systematic determination of merit, worth, and significance of something or someone using criteria against a set of standards. _____ often is used to characterize and appraise subjects of interest in a wide range of human enterprises, including the arts, criminal justice, foundations and non-profit organizations, government, health care, and other human services.

Depending on the topic of interest, there are professional groups which look to the quality and rigor of the _____ process.

   a. ACNielsen
   b. Evaluation
   c. AMAX
   d. ADTECH

Chapter 5. Qualitative Sales Forecasting

9. A _____ or logistics network is the system of organizations, people, technology, activities, information and resources involved in moving a product or service from supplier to customer. _____ activities transform natural resources, raw materials and components into a finished product that is delivered to the end customer. In sophisticated _____ systems, used products may re-enter the _____ at any point where residual value is recyclable.
   a. Supply chain network
   b. Demand chain management
   c. Purchasing
   d. Supply chain

10. _____ in economics and business is the result of an exchange and from that trade we assign a numerical monetary value to a good, service or asset. If I trade 4 apples for an orange, the _____ of an orange is 4 - apples. Inversely, the _____ of an apple is 1/4 oranges.
    a. Price
    b. Contribution margin-based pricing
    c. Discounts and allowances
    d. Pricing

11. _____ involves disseminating information about a product, product line, brand, or company. It is one of the four key aspects of the marketing mix. (The other three elements are product marketing, pricing, and distribution). P>_____ is generally sub-divided into two parts:

    - Above the line _____: Promotion in the media (e.g. TV, radio, newspapers, Internet and Mobile Phones) in which the advertiser pays an advertising agency to place the ad
    - Below the line _____: All other _____. Much of this is intended to be subtle enough for the consumer to be unaware that _____ is taking place. E.g. sponsorship, product placement, endorsements, sales _____, merchandising, direct mail, personal selling, public relations, trade shows

    a. Davie Brown Index
    b. Bottling lines
    c. Cashmere Agency
    d. Promotion

12. _____ often refers to either primary or secondary research. Secondary research involves a company using information compiled from various sources, which is about a new or existing product. The advantages of secondary research are that it is relatively cheap and easily accessible.

a. Market research
b. Mystery shopping
c. Questionnaire
d. Mystery shoppers

13. _____ refer to a collection of facts usually collected as the result of experience, observation or experiment or a set of premises. This may consist of numbers, words particularly as measurements or observations of a set of variables. _____ are often viewed as a lowest level of abstraction from which information and knowledge are derived.
    a. Sample size
    b. Pearson product-moment correlation coefficient
    c. Mean
    d. Data

14. In statistics, _____ has two related meanings:

    - the arithmetic _____
    - the expected value of a random variable, which is also called the population _____.

It is sometimes stated that the '_____' _____s average. This is incorrect if '_____' is taken in the specific sense of 'arithmetic _____' as there are different types of averages: the _____, median, and mode. For instance, average house prices almost always use the median value for the average. These three types of averages are all measures of locations.

   a. Standard normal distribution
   b. Heteroskedastic
   c. Confidence interval
   d. Mean

15. _____ is a term for unprocessed data, it is also known as primary data. It is a relative term _____ can be input to a computer program or used in manual analysis procedures such as gathering statistics from a survey.
    a. Product manager
    b. Chief marketing officer
    c. Shoppers Food ' Pharmacy
    d. Raw data

16. A _____ is a form of qualitative research in which a group of people are asked about their attitude towards a product, service, concept, advertisement, idea, or packaging. Questions are asked in an interactive group setting where participants are free to talk with other group members.

Chapter 5. Qualitative Sales Forecasting

Ernest Dichter originated the idea of having a 'group therapy' for products and this process is what became known as a _____.

a. Cross tabulation
b. Marketing research process
c. Logit analysis
d. Focus group

17. _____s is the social science that studies the production, distribution, and consumption of goods and services. The term _____s comes from the Ancient Greek oá¼°κονομῖα from oá¼¶κος (oikos, 'house') + vϾμος (nomos, 'custom' or 'law'), hence 'rules of the house(hold)'. Current _____ models developed out of the broader field of political economy in the late 19th century, owing to a desire to use an empirical approach more akin to the physical sciences.

a. ACNielsen
b. Economic
c. Industrial organization
d. ADTECH

18. An _____ is a statistic about the economy. _____s allow analysis of economic performance and predictions of future performance.

_____s include various indices, earnings reports, and economic summaries, such as unemployment, housing starts, Consumer Price Index (a measure for inflation), industrial production, bankruptcies, Gross Domestic Product, broadband internet penetration, retail sales, stock market prices, and money supply changes.

a. ADTECH
b. ACNielsen
c. Economic indicator
d. AMAX

19. Combining Existing _____ Sources with New Primary Data Sources

Imagine that we could get hold of a good collection of surveys taken in earlier years, such as detailed studies about changes going on in this phase and hopefully additional studies in the years to come. Analyzing this data base over time could give us a good picture of what changes actually have taken place in the orientation of the population and of the extent to which new technical concepts did have an impact on subgroups of the population. Furthermore, data archives can help to prepare studies on change over time by monitoring what questions have been asked in earlier years and alerting principal investigators to important questions which should be repeated in planned research projects.

a. 180SearchAssistant
b. 6-3-5 Brainwriting
c. Secondary Data
d. Power III

20. _____ is the imitation of some real thing, state of affairs, or process. The act of simulating something generally entails representing certain key characteristics or behaviors of a selected physical or abstract system.

_____ is used in many contexts, including the modeling of natural systems or human systems in order to gain insight into their functioning.

a. 6-3-5 Brainwriting
b. 180SearchAssistant
c. Power III
d. Simulation

Chapter 6. Sales Forecasting Systems

1. _____ is the process of estimation in unknown situations. Prediction is a similar, but more general term. Both can refer to estimation of time series, cross-sectional or longitudinal data.
   a. Power III
   b. 6-3-5 Brainwriting
   c. 180SearchAssistant
   d. Forecasting

2. _____ refer to a collection of facts usually collected as the result of experience, observation or experiment or a set of premises. This may consist of numbers, words particularly as measurements or observations of a set of variables. _____ are often viewed as a lowest level of abstraction from which information and knowledge are derived.
   a. Pearson product-moment correlation coefficient
   b. Mean
   c. Sample size
   d. Data

3. A _____ is a commercial building for storage of goods. _____s are used by manufacturers, importers, exporters, wholesalers, transport businesses, customs, etc. They are usually large plain buildings in industrial areas of cities and towns.
   a. 6-3-5 Brainwriting
   b. Warehouse
   c. 180SearchAssistant
   d. Power III

4. _____ is a recursive process where two or more people or organizations work together toward an intersection of common goals -- for example, an intellectual endeavor that is creative in nature--by sharing knowledge, learning and building consensus. _____ does not require leadership and can sometimes bring better results through decentralization and egalitarianism. In particular, teams that work collaboratively can obtain greater resources, recognition and reward when facing competition for finite resources. _____ is also present in opposing goals exhibiting the notion of adversarial _____, though this notion is atypical of the annotation that people have given towards their understanding of _____.
   a. Collaboration
   b. 6-3-5 Brainwriting
   c. 180SearchAssistant
   d. Power III

5. On an intranet or B2E Enterprise Web portals, personalization is often based on user attributes such as department, functional area, or role. The term _____ in this context refers to the ability of users to modify the page layout or specify what content should be displayed.

Chapter 6. Sales Forecasting Systems

There are two categories of personalizations:

1. Rule-based
2. Content-based

Web personalization models include rules-based filtering, based on 'if this, then that' rules processing, and collaborative filtering, which serves relevant material to customers by combining their own personal preferences with the preferences of like-minded others. Collaborative filtering works well for books, music, video, etc.

   a. Customization
   b. Movin'
   c. Cashmere Agency
   d. Self branding

6. _____ in organizations and public policy is both the organizational process of creating and maintaining a plan; and the psychological process of thinking about the activities required to create a desired goal on some scale. As such, it is a fundamental property of intelligent behavior. This thought process is essential to the creation and refinement of a plan, or integration of it with other plans, that is, it combines forecasting of developments with the preparation of scenarios of how to react to them.
   a. 6-3-5 Brainwriting
   b. 180SearchAssistant
   c. Planning
   d. Power III

7. The _____ is a systematic, interactive forecasting method which relies on a panel of independent experts. The carefully selected experts answer questionnaires in two or more rounds. After each round, a facilitator provides an anonymous summary of the experts' forecasts from the previous round as well as the reasons they provided for their judgments.
   a. Power III
   b. 180SearchAssistant
   c. Delphi method
   d. Futurist

8. In statistics, _____ is a collective name for techniques for the modeling and analysis of numerical data consisting of values of a dependent variable and of one or more independent variables The dependent variable in the regression equation is modeled as a function of the independent variables, corresponding parameters, and an error term. The error term is treated as a random variable.

a. Stepwise regression
b. Multicollinearity
c. Variance inflation factor
d. Regression analysis

9. In statistics, _____ has two related meanings:

   - the arithmetic _____
   - the expected value of a random variable, which is also called the population _____.

It is sometimes stated that the '_____' _____s average. This is incorrect if '_____' is taken in the specific sense of 'arithmetic _____' as there are different types of averages: the _____, median, and mode. For instance, average house prices almost always use the median value for the average. These three types of averages are all measures of locations.

a. Mean
b. Heteroskedastic
c. Standard normal distribution
d. Confidence interval

Chapter 7. Benchmark Studies: The Surveys

1. _____ is the process of estimation in unknown situations. Prediction is a similar, but more general term. Both can refer to estimation of time series, cross-sectional or longitudinal data.
   a. Power III
   b. Forecasting
   c. 6-3-5 Brainwriting
   d. 180SearchAssistant

2. _____ is a broad label that refers to any individuals or households that use goods and services generated within the economy. The concept of a _____ is used in different contexts, so that the usage and significance of the term may vary.

   A _____ is a person who uses any product or service.

   a. 180SearchAssistant
   b. 6-3-5 Brainwriting
   c. Power III
   d. Consumer

3. The _____ is a systematic, interactive forecasting method which relies on a panel of independent experts. The carefully selected experts answer questionnaires in two or more rounds. After each round, a facilitator provides an anonymous summary of the experts' forecasts from the previous round as well as the reasons they provided for their judgments.
   a. Futurist
   b. Delphi method
   c. 180SearchAssistant
   d. Power III

4. The general definition of an _____ is an evaluation of a person, organization, system, process, project or product. _____s are performed to ascertain the validity and reliability of information; also to provide an assessment of a system's internal control. The goal of an _____ is to express an opinion on the person/organization/system (etc) in question, under evaluation based on work done on a test basis.
   a. Audit
   b. ADTECH
   c. AMAX
   d. ACNielsen

Chapter 7. Benchmark Studies: The Surveys   31

5. _____ refers to the structured transmission of data between organizations by electronic means. It is used to transfer electronic documents from one computer system to another (ie) from one trading partner to another trading partner. It is more than mere E-mail; for instance, organizations might replace bills of lading and even checks with appropriate _____ messages.
   a. AMAX
   b. ADTECH
   c. ACNielsen
   d. Electronic data interchange

6. _____ is a family of business models in which the buyer of a product provides certain information to a supplier of that product and the supplier takes full responsibility for maintaining an agreed inventory of the material, usually at the buyer's consumption location (usually a store.) A third party logistics provider can also be involved to make sure that the buyer have the required level of inventory by adjusting the demand and supply gaps.

As a symbiotic relationship, _____ makes it less likely that a business will unintentionally become out of stock of a good and reduces inventory in the supply chain.

   a. Merchandise management system
   b. Vendor Managed Inventory
   c. Reverse auction
   d. Customer driven supply chain

7. _____ refer to a collection of facts usually collected as the result of experience, observation or experiment or a set of premises. This may consist of numbers, words particularly as measurements or observations of a set of variables. _____ are often viewed as a lowest level of abstraction from which information and knowledge are derived.
   a. Sample size
   b. Data
   c. Pearson product-moment correlation coefficient
   d. Mean

8. _____ is a list for goods and materials held available in stock by a business. It is also used for a list of the contents of a household and for a list for testamentary purposes of the possessions of someone who has died. In accounting _____ is considered an asset.
   a. Ending Inventory
   b. ACNielsen
   c. ADTECH
   d. Inventory

Chapter 8. Benchmark Studies: World-Class Forecasting

1. In economics, _____ is the desire to own something and the ability to pay for it. The term _____ signifies the ability or the willingness to buy a particular commodity at a given point of time .

    a. Market dominance
    b. Discretionary spending
    c. Market system
    d. Demand

2. _____ is the process of estimation in unknown situations. Prediction is a similar, but more general term. Both can refer to estimation of time series, cross-sectional or longitudinal data.
    a. Power III
    b. Forecasting
    c. 6-3-5 Brainwriting
    d. 180SearchAssistant

3. _____ is the process whereby an organization establishes the parameters within which programs, investments, and acquisitions are reaching the desired results. Performance Reference Model of the Federal Enterprise Architecture, 2005.

    This process of measuring performance often requires the use of statistical evidence to determine progress toward specific defined organizational objectives.

    There are many types of measurements.

    a. Crisis management
    b. Performance measurement
    c. Digital strategy
    d. Voice of the customer

4. In statistics, _____ has two related meanings:

    - the arithmetic _____
    - the expected value of a random variable, which is also called the population _____.

    It is sometimes stated that the '_____' _____s average. This is incorrect if '_____' is taken in the specific sense of 'arithmetic _____' as there are different types of averages: the _____, median, and mode. For instance, average house prices almost always use the median value for the average. These three types of averages are all measures of locations.

a. Mean
b. Standard normal distribution
c. Confidence interval
d. Heteroskedastic

5. The general definition of an _____ is an evaluation of a person, organization, system, process, project or product. _____s are performed to ascertain the validity and reliability of information; also to provide an assessment of a system's internal control. The goal of an _____ is to express an opinion on the person/organization/system (etc) in question, under evaluation based on work done on a test basis.
   a. ACNielsen
   b. AMAX
   c. ADTECH
   d. Audit

6. In probability theory and statistics, _____ indicates the strength and direction of a linear relationship between two random variables. That is in contrast with the usage of the term in colloquial speech, denoting any relationship, not necessarily linear. In general statistical usage, _____ or co-relation refers to the departure of two random variables from independence.
   a. Mean
   b. Probability
   c. Frequency distribution
   d. Correlation

Chapter 9. Benchmark Studies: Conducting a Forecasting Audit

1. The general definition of an _____ is an evaluation of a person, organization, system, process, project or product. _____s are performed to ascertain the validity and reliability of information; also to provide an assessment of a system's internal control. The goal of an _____ is to express an opinion on the person/organization/system (etc) in question, under evaluation based on work done on a test basis.
    a. ACNielsen
    b. AMAX
    c. ADTECH
    d. Audit

2. A _____ is a formal statement of a set of business goals, the reasons why they are believed attainable, and the plan for reaching those goals. It may also contain background information about the organization or team attempting to reach those goals.

    The business goals may be defined for for-profit or for non-profit organizations.

    a. Digital strategy
    b. Logistics management
    c. Business plan
    d. Product marketing

3. _____ is the process of estimation in unknown situations. Prediction is a similar, but more general term. Both can refer to estimation of time series, cross-sectional or longitudinal data.
    a. Power III
    b. 180SearchAssistant
    c. 6-3-5 Brainwriting
    d. Forecasting

4. In statistics and image processing, to smooth a data set is to create an approximating function that attempts to capture important patterns in the data, while leaving out noise or other fine-scale structures/rapid phenomena. Many different algorithms are used in _____. One of the most common algorithms is the 'moving average', often used to try to capture important trends in repeated statistical surveys.
    a. Smoothing
    b. 6-3-5 Brainwriting
    c. Power III
    d. 180SearchAssistant

5. _____ is the process whereby an organization establishes the parameters within which programs, investments, and acquisitions are reaching the desired results. Performance Reference Model of the Federal Enterprise Architecture, 2005.

Chapter 9. Benchmark Studies: Conducting a Forecasting Audit

This process of measuring performance often requires the use of statistical evidence to determine progress toward specific defined organizational objectives.

There are many types of measurements.

a. Digital strategy
b. Crisis management
c. Voice of the customer
d. Performance measurement

Chapter 10. Managing the Sales Forecasting Function

1. _____ is the process of estimation in unknown situations. Prediction is a similar, but more general term. Both can refer to estimation of time series, cross-sectional or longitudinal data.
   a. 180SearchAssistant
   b. Power III
   c. 6-3-5 Brainwriting
   d. Forecasting

2. _____ is defined by the American _____ Association as the activity, set of institutions, and processes for creating, communicating, delivering, and exchanging offerings that have value for customers, clients, partners, and society at large. The term developed from the original meaning which referred literally to going to market, as in shopping, or going to a market to sell goods or services.

   _____ practice tends to be seen as a creative industry, which includes advertising, distribution and selling.

   a. Customer acquisition management
   b. Marketing myopia
   c. Product naming
   d. Marketing

3. A _____ is a written document that details the necessary actions to achieve one or more marketing objectives. It can be for a product or service, a brand, or a product line. _____s cover between one and five years.
   a. Disruptive technology
   b. Prosumer
   c. Marketing plan
   d. Marketing strategy

4. The general definition of an _____ is an evaluation of a person, organization, system, process, project or product. _____s are performed to ascertain the validity and reliability of information; also to provide an assessment of a system's internal control. The goal of an _____ is to express an opinion on the person/organization/system (etc) in question, under evaluation based on work done on a test basis.
   a. AMAX
   b. ADTECH
   c. ACNielsen
   d. Audit

5. In economics, business, retail, and accounting, a _____ is the value of money that has been used up to produce something, and hence is not available for use anymore. In economics, a _____ is an alternative that is given up as a result of a decision. In business, the _____ may be one of acquisition, in which case the amount of money expended to acquire it is counted as _____.

Chapter 10. Managing the Sales Forecasting Function

a. Variable cost
b. Fixed costs
c. Transaction cost
d. Cost

6. The _____ is a systematic, interactive forecasting method which relies on a panel of independent experts. The carefully selected experts answer questionnaires in two or more rounds. After each round, a facilitator provides an anonymous summary of the experts' forecasts from the previous round as well as the reasons they provided for their judgments.

a. Power III
b. 180SearchAssistant
c. Futurist
d. Delphi method

7. A _____ attribute is one that exists in a range of magnitudes, and can therefore be measured. Measurements of any particular _____ property are expressed as a specific quantity, referred to as a unit, multiplied by a number. Examples of physical quantities are distance, mass, and time.

a. BeyondROI
b. Lifestyle city
c. Dolly Dimples
d. Quantitative

8. In economics, _____ is the desire to own something and the ability to pay for it. The term _____ signifies the ability or the willingness to buy a particular commodity at a given point of time .

a. Discretionary spending
b. Demand
c. Market dominance
d. Market system

9. In economics, _____' is the art or science of controlling economic demand to avoid a recession. In natural resources management and environmental policy more generally, it refers to policies to control consumer demand for environmentally sensitive or harmful goods such as water and energy. Within manufacturing firms the term is used to describe the activities of demand forecasting, planning and order fulfillment.

Chapter 10. Managing the Sales Forecasting Function

a. Demand management
b. Power III
c. 6-3-5 Brainwriting
d. 180SearchAssistant

10. In probability theory and statistics, _____ indicates the strength and direction of a linear relationship between two random variables. That is in contrast with the usage of the term in colloquial speech, denoting any relationship, not necessarily linear. In general statistical usage, _____ or co-relation refers to the departure of two random variables from independence.
   a. Probability
   b. Frequency distribution
   c. Correlation
   d. Mean

11. In statistics, _____ is a collective name for techniques for the modeling and analysis of numerical data consisting of values of a dependent variable and of one or more independent variables The dependent variable in the regression equation is modeled as a function of the independent variables, corresponding parameters, and an error term. The error term is treated as a random variable.
   a. Variance inflation factor
   b. Multicollinearity
   c. Stepwise regression
   d. Regression analysis

12. A mutual _____ or stockholder is an individual or company (including a corporation) that legally owns one or more shares of stock in a joint stock company. A company's _____s collectively own that company. Thus, the typical goal of such companies is to enhance _____ value.
   a. 180SearchAssistant
   b. Power III
   c. Shareholder
   d. Total shareholder return

13. _____ is a business buzz term, which implies that the ultimate measure of a company's success is to enrich shareholders. It became popular during the 1980s, and is particularly associated with former CEO of General Electric, Jack Welch. In March 2009, Welch openly turned his back on the concept, calling shardeholder value 'the dumbest idea in the world'.

Chapter 10. Managing the Sales Forecasting Function 39

   a. Shareholder value
   b. 180SearchAssistant
   c. Power III
   d. 6-3-5 Brainwriting

14. A personal and cultural _____ is a relative ethic _____, an assumption upon which implementation can be extrapolated. A _____ system is a set of consistent _____s and measures that is soo not true. A principle _____ is a foundation upon which other _____s and measures of integrity are based.
   a. Package-on-Package
   b. Supreme Court of the United States
   c. Perceptual maps
   d. Value

15. In statistics and image processing, to smooth a data set is to create an approximating function that attempts to capture important patterns in the data, while leaving out noise or other fine-scale structures/rapid phenomena. Many different algorithms are used in _____. One of the most common algorithms is the 'moving average', often used to try to capture important trends in repeated statistical surveys.
   a. 180SearchAssistant
   b. 6-3-5 Brainwriting
   c. Power III
   d. Smoothing

ANSWER KEY

Chapter 1
1. d   2. d   3. d   4. d   5. d   6. b   7. d   8. b   9. d   10. b
11. b   12. d   13. c   14. c   15. c   16. b   17. d   18. b   19. a   20. d
21. d

Chapter 2
1. d   2. b   3. b   4. d   5. d   6. d   7. b   8. d   9. d   10. c
11. d   12. d   13. b   14. d   15. b

Chapter 3
1. d   2. d   3. a   4. c   5. d   6. c   7. a   8. d

Chapter 4
1. b   2. d   3. d   4. d   5. d   6. c   7. d   8. d   9. a   10. c
11. b   12. d   13. d   14. a   15. b   16. d   17. c   18. b

Chapter 5
1. b   2. c   3. d   4. d   5. d   6. d   7. b   8. b   9. d   10. a
11. d   12. a   13. d   14. d   15. d   16. d   17. b   18. c   19. c   20. d

Chapter 6
1. d   2. d   3. b   4. a   5. a   6. c   7. c   8. d   9. a

Chapter 7
1. b   2. d   3. b   4. a   5. d   6. b   7. b   8. d

Chapter 8
1. d   2. b   3. b   4. a   5. d   6. d

Chapter 9
1. d   2. c   3. d   4. a   5. d

Chapter 10
1. d   2. d   3. c   4. d   5. d   6. d   7. d   8. b   9. a   10. c
11. d   12. c   13. a   14. d   15. d

www.ingramcontent.com/pod-product-compliance
Lightning Source LLC
Chambersburg PA
CBHW081220230426
43666CB00015B/2822